# BACKGAMMON FOR WINNERS

## Bill Robertie

- Gambling Research Institute -
## Cardoza Publishing

## ABOUT THE AUTHOR

Bill Robertie is the world's best backgammon player and the only two-time winner of the Monte Carlo World Championships. He is the author of four advanced books on winning at backgammon and the co-publisher of *Inside Backgammon*, the world's foremost backgammon magazine. He's also a chess master and a winner of the U.S. Speed Chess Championship.

His club and tournament winnings have allowed him to travel the world in style. Robertie currently makes his home in Arlington, Massachusetts.

Other Books by Bill Robertie
Advanced Backgammon Volume 1: Positional Play
Advanced Backgammon Volume 2: Technical Play
Lee Genud vs. Joe Dwek
Reno 1986

*First Edition*

Library of Congress Catalog Card No: 93-70982          ISBN: 0-940685-42-6
• Front Cover Photo by Ron Charles

**Cardoza Publishing**, publisher of **Gambling Research Institute** (GRI) books, is the foremost gaming and gambling publisher in the world with a library of more than 50 up-to-date and easy-to-read books and strategies.

These authoritative works are written by the top experts in their fields and with more than 3,500,000 books in print, represent the best-selling and most popular gaming books anywhere.

**Write for your free catalogue of gambling books, advanced strategies and computer games**

CARDOZA PUBLISHING
P.O. Box 1500, Cooper Station, New York, NY 10276 • (718)743-5229

# Table of Contents

# I. INTRODUCTION

Welcome to backgammon - the world's most exciting game!

In this book, you'll learn all about backgammon, from how to set up a board and the basics of play, to the winning strategies that not only can make you a better player, but can win you money! Backgammon is a great game when played for fun, and that's how many people like to play it. It's even more fun when it's played for money and the doubling cube takes on more significance.

While backgammon's easy to learn and a single game can be played in about 10 minutes, the strategies can be complex. The landscape of battle is constantly in motion and every roll brings new challenges, new dangers and new opportunities. And until the game is actually over, there's always the possibilities of incredible swings of fortunes.

I'm going to show you how to play my style - *dynamic backgammon* - the winning strategy based on aggressive play. It's a daring way to play, a style where chances are taken early to reap big rewards later, but a style that allows you to take control of the game and be a winner.

I'll show you how a well-constructed opening plan can pave the way to a decisive victory. You'll not only learn the best way to play all opening moves so that you can get an advantage right from the beginning, but the secrets that the world's top players use to bulldoze their opponents: duplication, blitzing, priming and doubling strategy.

To illustrate and make the strategies crystal clear, we've included two complete games, with diagrams and comments after nearly every move. We'll follow the thinking and play of each situation so that by the time you finish this book, you'll have the skills to be a winner at backgammon.

The luckiest thing I ever did in my life was learn how to play backgammon. That's a move you're about to make, and I hope it's just as lucky for you too.

# II. THE BASICS OF PLAY

## Introduction
Most board games fall into one of two general types: the **war games,** or games of maneuver, encirclement and capture (chess and checkers are the most popular examples), and **race games** such as backgammon, where the objective is to outrace your opponent around some sort of track or layout.

Backgammon is by far the most popular of the race games. Each player has an army of 15 pieces, also called **checkers** or **men,** which move around a board consisting of 24 triangular **points**. The points are similar to squares on a chessboard, except that each point can hold any number of men from the same army.

## The Players
Backgammon is played by two opposing players, but unlike chess or checkers, it makes no difference what color pieces you play - either color is equally likely to make the first move.

## The Equipment
To play backgammon, you need the following equipment:

• A backgammon board.

• Thirty round checkers, fifteen each of two different colors. The checkers are often referred to as **men** or **pieces.**

• Two pairs of dice. Usually, dice with rounded corners are used, although this is not strictly necessary.

• Two dice cups, for shaking and throwing the dice. The best dice cups have a small lip, or raised surface just inside the mouth of the cup to guarantee that the dice are rolling when they leave the cup.

• **A doubling cube,** a six-sided cube with the numbers 2, 4, 8, 16, 32 and 64 on the six faces. This keeps track of the number of units at stake in the game.

## The Backgammon Board

Backgammon boards vary widely in price and quality. You can buy an inexpensive board at your local game department store for just a few dollars. You can spend about $100 and get a full tournament-sized set with a playing surface of cork or cloth. Or, if you're feeling wealthy or just extravagant, you can spend over $1000 for beautiful leather boards with contrasting leather and brass accessories.

Most backgammon sets fold in half for convenience. Clubs, however, sometimes purchase solid sets made from one piece of wood. And some sets are even inlaid into table tops. Whatever your choice, you should invest in a backgammon set and use it to play along with the examples in this book. You'll find that learning the concepts is much easier if you actually take the time to move real pieces about on a real board.

Diagram 1 shows a backgammon board, with each point numbered 1- 24.

### Diagram 1: A Backgammon Board

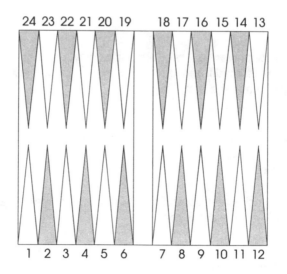

The board is divided into four sections, or **quadrants**, with six points in each quadrant. Running down through the middle of the board is a raised section known as the **bar**. The bar is not a point but instead, is a resting place for checkers that have been **hit**, or captured, during the course of play. Once a checker has been hit, it is placed on the bar, and must first reenter in the farthest quadrant before any other pieces can move.

## How to Set Up the Board

Diagram 2 shows the initial placement of the pieces at the beginning of the game. Black has two pieces on the point labelled **24**, three pieces on point **8**, and five pieces on points **6** and **13**. White's position is the mirror image of Black's. He has two checkers on point **1**, three on point **17**, and five each on points **12** and **19**.

### Diagram 2: Starting Position

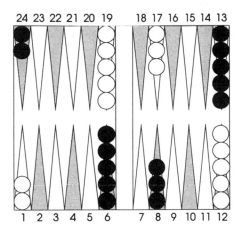

## The Direction of Movement

The two armies race around the board in opposite directions. Diagram 3 shows the direction of movement of the two armies.

8

**Diagram 3: Direction of Movement**

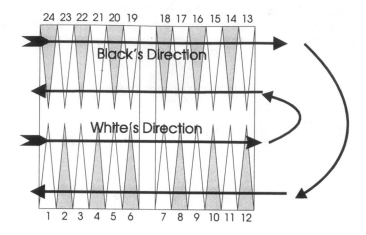

Black checkers move in a clockwise direction, from the upper left to the upper right quadrants, then down to the lower right quadrant and finally to the lower left quadrant. The White checkers move in the opposite direction.

Notice that the top and bottom halves of the board are connected along the right-hand side: a Black piece moving to the point numbered 13 in the diagram moves next to the point numbered 12, and then along to 11 and so forth. A White piece moving along the bottom of the board to point 12 will next move to point 13, and then to the left along the top edge of the board.

### How To Move The Pieces
In backgammon, the two players take turns moving. To make a move, a player puts two dice in his cup, shakes them, and rolls the dice out onto the right-hand side of the board. He then moves his checkers corresponding to the numbers on the dice.

Suppose, for instance, it is your turn and you roll a 3 and a 1. You can move two separate checkers, or you can make your whole move with one checker. You may move one checker three spaces forward and another checker one space forward, or one checker a total of four spaces forward. This is not quite the same as having a move of four spaces as we shall see, for each die must be played individually.

Look at Diagram 4. Black has a 3-1 to play. (Remember that Black moves clockwise around the board). He elects to move one checker from the 13-point to the 10-point (a total of three spaces) and another checker from the 24-point to the 23-point (one space). The resulting position is shown in Diagram 5.

Diagram 4: Black to play a 3-1

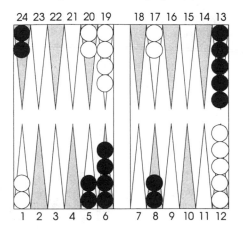

Diagram 5: Position after Black has played 13 to 10 and 24 to 23

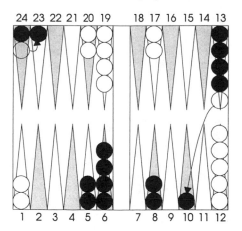

In Diagram 6, White has a 4-2 to play. He elects to move one checker four spaces from the 17-point to the 21-point (White moves in the opposite direction from Black) and one checker two spaces from the 19-point to the 21-point. Diagram 7 shows the position after White has played the 4-2.

Diagram 6: White has a 4-2 to play

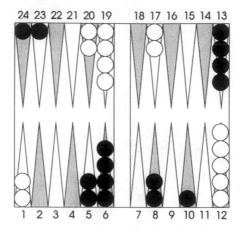

Diagram 7: White has played the 4-2

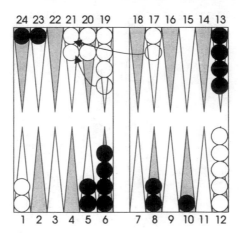

**Doubles**

Up to now we've looked at what happens when you throw two different numbers on the dice. Suppose, however, that the same number comes up on both dice? That's called throwing **doubles**, and it's very good for you.

When you throw doubles, you get to play the number, not just twice, but four times! In most positions, this gives you a powerful jump on your opponent, and in fact, if you throw more doubles than your opponent, you will probably win the game.

**Diagram 8: Black to play 44**

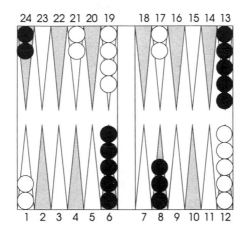

In Diagram 8, Black has thrown double-4s. He has many ways to play the number, all of which are good for him. One of the best is to use two of his 4s to bring both men from the 24-point to the 20-point, and the other two 4s to bring two men from the 13-point to the 9-point. The resulting position is shown in Diagram 9.

Diagram 9: Position after Black plays 44

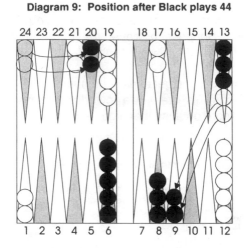

## Points

Two checkers of the same color on a point constitute a **made point**, or simply a **point**. The opposing player cannot land on that point by an exact count, although he may hop over the point and move beyond it.

Diagram 10: Black to play 53

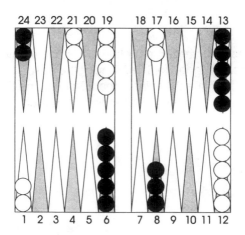

Look at Position 10. Black has a 5-3 to play. Notice that he cannot move either of the checkers on the 24-point. He can't move them 3 spaces, because the point 3 spaces away is the 21-point, and White has made that point with two of his checkers. He also can't move the checkers 5 spaces, because the point 5 spaces away is the 19-point, and White has made that point with four of his checkers. So the checkers on the 24-point can't move either part of the roll, although the point 8 spaces away, the 16-point, is still wide open.

Several points in a row constitute a **prime**. Six points in a row is a **full prime**, and any checkers caught behind a full prime are trapped until the prime is broken.

You must always play both parts of your throw if you can. Take a look at Diagram 11. Black has a 6-4 to play. Notice that if Black plays his 4 first, from 24 to 20, then he has no 6 to play anywhere on the board! This isn't legal. Black could play either 24 to 18 and 13 to 9, or 13 to 9 to 3. But he must use his whole throw if he can.

**Diagram 11: Black has a 6 and 4 to play**

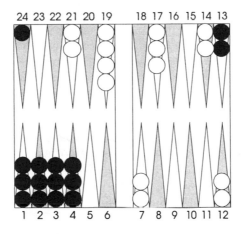

Sometimes a position arises where a player can play one number or the other, but not both. Look at Diagram 12.

**Diagram 12: Black to play 65**

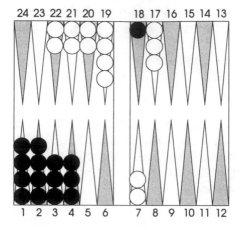

Black has a 6 and a 5 to play. If he plays the 6, he will have no legal 5, but if he plays the 5, he will have no 6! In this case, Black **must** play the larger of the two numbers. His only legal play is from 18 to 12, stopping there.

## Blots

A **blot** is a single checker on a point. While two men on a point constitute a strong fortress that can restrain an opponent, a blot is a vulnerable weakness, which can be hit and sent back to the beginning of the race.

Look at Diagram 13.

Diagram 13

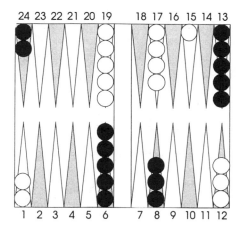

White has a blot on the 15-point. Black now rolls a 6-3. He can take one of his checkers on the 24-point, move it to the 15-point using his entire roll, and *hit* the White blot. The White blot now moves from the 15-point to the *bar* (the raised area in the center of the board). The resulting position is shown in Diagram 14.

Diagram 14. Position after White has been hit

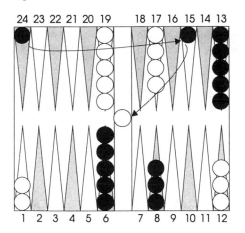

## Entering From the Bar

The bar is a sort of holding pen, where White and Black checkers that have been hit are placed to restart their race around the board. Once a checker is on the bar, no other checker can be moved until that checker has been reentered onto the board. White's checkers must enter in Black's home board (points 1- 6). Black's checkers enter in White's home board (points 24-19).

Let's look at Diagram 14 again. White has been sent to the bar and must now enter before he can make any move with his other pieces. Suppose his next roll is a 2-6. This gives him a 2 and a 6 to play. He could use the 2 to enter his checker from the bar to the 2-point, which is open.

But notice that he can't use the 6 to enter, because the 6-point is a made point and belongs to Black. So half of White's move is forced - he has to use his 2 to place the checker from the bar to the 2-point. He can now make any legal 6 he wishes. Suppose he plays a checker from the 1-point to the 7-point. The resulting position is shown in Diagram 15.

**Diagram 15. Position after White played 62**

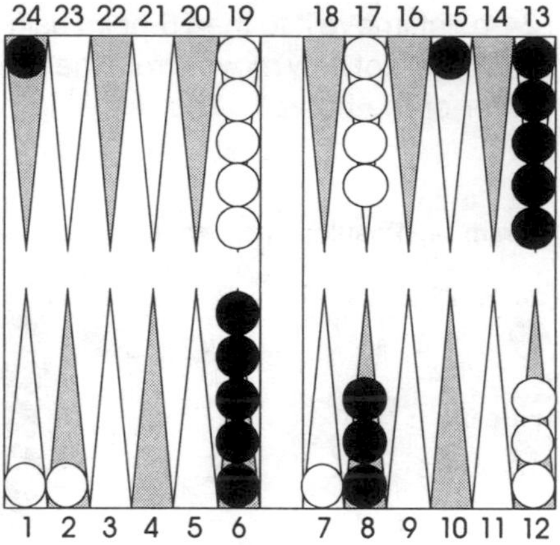

## The Opening Roll

To begin the game, each player puts one die in his cup, shakes it, and rolls the die out into his right-hand half of the board. The player who throws the larger number moves first, and his roll is the combination of the two dice. For example: you and I are playing. You roll a five, and I roll a three. You have the opening roll, and you must play a 5-3.

Some players play with the rule of **automatic doubles**: if both players roll the same number on the opening throw, the cube is turned to 2 and the players roll again. However, this is an optional rule.

## The Object of the Game
When playing backgammon, your objective is to take all your checkers off the board before your opponent. Before you can take any checkers off the board, however, you must first maneuver all your checkers into your own *inner board*. In the diagrams that we've been using, the points labelled 1 through 6 are *Black's inner board* or *home*, while the points labelled 19 through 24 are *White's inner board* or *home*.

Once all 15 of your checkers are in your own inner board, you may begin *bearing off*. (See explanation below). If you bear off all your checkers before your opponent, but your opponent gets at least one checker off, you win a *single game*, worth 1 point. If you bear off all your checkers before your opponent bears off any checkers, you win a **gammon**, or **double game**, worth 2 points. And, if you bear off all your checkers and your opponent still has one or more checkers on the bar or in your inner board, you win a **backgammon**, or **triple game**, worth 3 points!

## Bearing Off
The object of the game is to bear all your checkers off the board before your opponent. However, you cannot bear off any checkers until all your checkers are in your *home board*.

**Diagram 16**

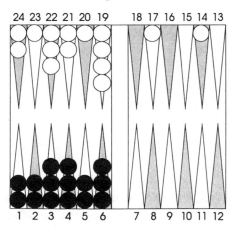

Black's home board are the points labelled 1- 6; White's home board are points 19 through 24. In Diagram 16, Black has already maneuvered all his men home. White, on the other hand, still has two men in his outer board. Black can start bearing off immediately; White still has to move those two outside men home.

To bear off, you roll the dice and remove men corresponding to the numbers thrown. For example, if Black throws a 5 and a 3 in Diagram 16, he may remove a checker from his 5-point and a checker from his 3-point. Once removed, a checker can never be returned to play.

You are not, however, compelled to remove checkers with the numbers thrown. With the 5-3 roll, Black could, if he wished, play a checker from his 6-point to his 1-point and a checker from his 5-point to his 2-point. However, this would not be as good as removing checkers from the board.

If you roll a number higher than the highest occupied point, you may use it to bear a checker off the highest occupied point. Look at Diagram 17.

**Diagram 17. Black to play 64**

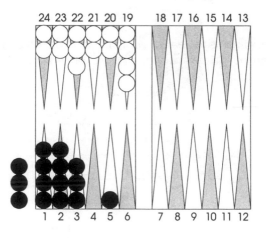

In this case, Black has no checkers on either the 6-point or the 4-point. He can use the 6 to bear off the checker from the 5-point, and then use the 4 to bear off his checker on the 3-point. If, in the process of bearing off, you leave a blot and your opponent hits you, you must first reenter that checker and bring it around to your home board before bearing off any other checkers. Look at Diagram 18.

**Diagram 18**

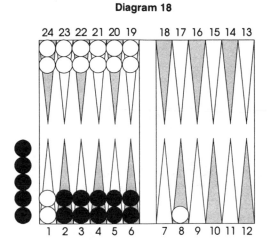

Black has been rolling well and has only 10 checkers left. White, on the other hand, is in bad shape. He's way behind, and might conceivably lose a gammon or a backgammon. Watch how quickly the tables can turn.

In Diagram 18, Black rolls 65. With the 6, he has to play a checker off the 6-point, leaving a vulnerable blot. With the 5, he would like to move that blot to a safe point, but he can't; the point five away from the 6-point is the 1-point, and White owns that. The only other play with the 5 is to take a checker off the 5-point, leaving another vulnerable blot! Look at Diagram 19.

**Diagram 19. Black has just played 65**

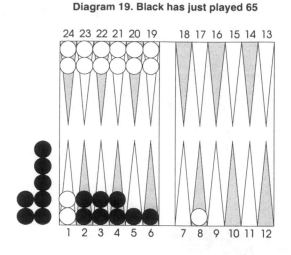

Black's left himself wide open and White pounces, rolling a 54! With the 5, he plays from the 1-point to the 6-point, hitting Black's blot and sending it to the bar. With the 4, he plays from the 1-point to the 5-point, hitting the other blot. The new position is shown in Diagram 20.

**Diagram 20. Black has two checkers on the bar**

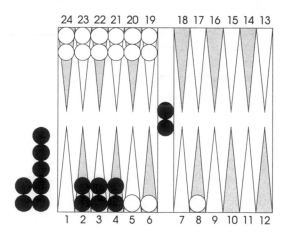

What can Black do? He has to enter checkers from the bar before he can move any others. But he has to enter in White's home board (the points numbered 19 through 24), and White owns all those points! No matter what number Black throws, it will correspond to a point that White has made. White's position is known as a **closed board**, and as long as White maintains this position, Black has no chance of entering and has to forfeit his turn.

The future course of this game is pretty clear. White will move his three remaining checkers around and in to his home board. Eventually, he will start removing checkers, and as he does, he will open up some of the points which he now controls. Once he does, Black can try to enter.

Even after Black enters both his men, however, he will have to move them around and back into his home board before he can start bearing off again. That's going to take a long time, however, so right now White is a big favorite to win the game. That's backgammon: a single stroke of bad luck (or good luck, depending on your point of view) can turn an apparently overwhelming position into a disaster.

### The Doubling Cube
In the 1920s, some unknown genius, probably living in the New York area, created something which forever changed the way backgammon was played: the **doubling cube**. With the addition of the doubling cube (backgammon players just refer to it as "the cube") backgammon became a quicker, more exciting game - the best two-player game in the world.

The doubling cube works like a raise in poker. If you like your position, you may raise the stakes, hoping to either drive the opposing player out of the game, or force him to accept a disadvantageous position at double the stakes.

The doubling cube is slightly larger than the dice used to determine the moves, and has the numbers 2, 4, 8, 16, 32 and 64 on its six sides. The cube is used to determine the value of the game (in a game played for money) or the number of points won or lost (in a tournament match).

At the beginning of a game, the doubling cube is placed between the two players with the number 64 facing up. Since there is no "1" on the cube, this indicates that the value of the game is currently 1 point. When one player feels that he has a solid advantage, he may choose to double the value of the game. He does this by saying *I double*, or something to that effect, and placing the cube on his opponent's side of the board with the number "2" facing up.

The second player now has a choice. He may feel he is a big underdog, and give up the game. In this case, he says *I drop*, and the game is finished. The player who doubled wins one point (the previous value of the cube).

Perhaps, however, the second player feels he still has a fighting chance to win. In this case he may say *I take*, or *I accept* and place the cube on his side of the board. He now *owns* the cube. The game continues, but the value of a single game is now doubled, 2 points. A gammon is now worth 4 points, and a backgammon is worth 6 points. Once the initial double has been made, only the player who owns the cube has the right to redouble.

Suppose that after some rolls, the second player feels that the position has turned in his favor. In this case he may, before he rolls the dice, redouble the game by turning the cube to 4 and offering it back to the first player. The first player may now give up the game and lose 2 points, or play on by accepting the cube at 4. In this case a single game is now worth 4 points, a gammon is worth 8 points, and a backgammon, 12 points!

Theoretically, this doubling and redoubling could continue for quite a while. In practice, between experienced players, the cube rarely gets beyond the 4 level. However, every veteran player has experienced a few games where the cube has reached 32 (or more)!

# III. DYNAMIC OPENINGS

## Introduction
In this section, we'll show you how to play dynamic backgammon so that right from the opening you're in control. **Dynamic play** lets you set the pace and determine the course the game will take. **Passive play**, on the other hand, lets your opponent call the shots. That's not what we want. In this section, we'll show you how to play your openings so you're in control.

Before we look at how to play particular rolls, however, we need to step back for a minute and consider the big picture. What are our goals in the opening? What are we trying to do?

## Winning Goals
Let's look again at Diagram 2, the starting position. Take a good look at Black's checkers. His goal, remember, is to maneuver all 15 of his checkers into his home board (points 1-6 in the diagram), then bear them off. And he needs to do all this before White does the same thing. Of his 15 checkers, five are already in his home board - the five located on the 6-point. Three others are close by, on the 8-point. And five others are located not too far away, on the 13-point.

These 13 checkers constitute the bulk of Black's army, and they don't have far to go to get home. What's more, because they're close to each other, they can cooperate in making new points. With a throw of 3-1, for instance, Black can move one checker from the 6-point and the 8-point to make the 5-point. In the same way, a throw of 4-2 will make the 4-point, and a throw of 6 -1 will make the 7-point (also known as the **bar-point**, because it's located right next to the bar in the middle of the board).

That's good news for those 13 checkers. They're close to home, and they support each other by being able to make new points. But what about Black's other two checkers?

Take a look at those other two checkers. They're stuck way back on the 24-point - a long way from the rest of Black's army. In order to connect with the rest of Black's forces, those checkers are going to have to make their way through a minefield - the 23 through the 14-points, an area which is pretty well controlled by **White's** army.

That, in a nutshell, is the real problem in the opening of a backgammon game - how to get your rear checkers forward to join the rest of your army, while White is doing his best to control their escape route and either hit them and send them back to the bar, or block their escape route by making new points. White, of course, has the very same problem. His rear checkers are trying to get out of your **home board**, through your **outer board** (the 7 through 12-points), and home to safety. The opening of most backgammon games is a constant seesaw struggle, with both players trying to simultaneously block and hit their opponent's men while mobilizing their own.

Here are the Four Key Opening Goals.

## Four Key Opening Goals
**1. Hit Your Opponent's Men** - This is key. When you can hit a checker, it's usually right to do it. Since your opponent's checker has to go to the bar and then reenter your home board *before he can do anything else*, you gain time in the race. If your opponent rolls some unlucky numbers, he might have to stay on the bar and lose a whole turn or two. That could give you time to escape with your backmen.

**2. Build Blocking Points** - This is very important, although usually a little less important than hitting your opponent. (But not always!) Every blocking point makes it more difficult for your opponent's back men to escape. The longer you can keep those back men trapped, the bigger your advantage.

**3. Build An Anchor** - What's an **anchor**, you ask? Answer: an advanced point in your opponent's home board. From Black's point of view, the 20-point, the 21-point, or the 18-point would constitute an anchor. If Black can move his two back men up to one of those points, he would have a strong defensive position which would be hard to block. Black could then bide his time and look for a chance to run home later.

**4. Mobilize Your Checkers** - By **mobilize**, I mean move your checkers into positions where they more easily accomplish goals 1-3. For instance, with a 4 on the dice you might move a back checker from the 24-point to the 20-point (hoping to make an anchor there next turn); with a 3 you might bring a checker from the 13-point to the 10-point (hoping to make a new blocking point the following turn). Since neither player has many dice throws on the opening turn to directly accomplish one of our first three goals, these *mobilization* plays are critical.

That's the overall picture. In the opening, you're trying to block, anchor, hit, and mobilize - **BAHM** for short. Now let's see how you'd play each of your 15 possible opening rolls. Remember, since you have to *win* the opening roll by throwing a bigger number than your opponent, you can't start the game with a double. Also, you can't do any hitting on the opening roll - in the starting position, neither you nor your opponent have any blots. (That situation will quickly change, however.)

# IV. THE OPENING MOVES

<u>The Blocking Rolls</u>: 3-1, 4-2, 5-3, and 6-1

### 3-1: Make the 5-point

The best opening shot is 3-1. Use it to make your 5-point, as in Diagram 21:

**Diagram 21. Black has played a 3-1**

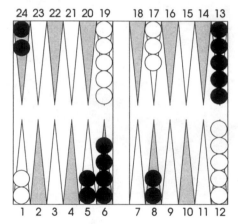

With this roll you accomplish two things: you make a blocking point, further hemming in White's two checkers on your 1-point, and you make an *inner-board point*.

The extra importance of an inner-board point (as opposed to a point in your outer board, like the 10-point) is simply this: if you hit your opponent at some point in the future, which you are likely to do, he will no longer be able to reenter the game when he throws a 5 on the dice, because that point now belongs to you.

Since you own the 6-point as well, your opponent will need to throw one of the numbers 1, 2, 3, or 4, to reenter from the bar. That may sound easy to do, but in fact by making that second point in your board, you quadrupled the number of dice throws that leave your opponent on the bar! When you only owned the 6-point, only one dice throw left White on the bar: 6-6. Now that you own the 5 and 6-points, a total of four throws will leave White on the bar: 6-6, 5-5, 6-5, and 5-6.

In the Middle East, where backgammon originated, inner points are called **doors**, because you have to enter through them to get back in the game. When *all* the doors are shut, you're closed out, and can't get back in the game.

### 4-2: Make the 4-point

The second-best opening roll is a 4-2, which you should use to make the 4-point, as in Diagram 22:

**Diagram 22: Black has played 4-2**

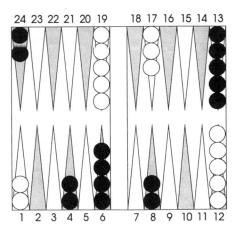

4-2 is a great opening roll for pretty much the same reasons as 3-1. It's not quite as good as 3-1 for this reason: after you make the 4-point, White still has a chance to sneak behind you and bring his back men up to the 5-point. If he can do that, the value of the 4-point will be somewhat negated.

This illustrates another important backgammon principle: *consecutive points are stronger than points with gaps in between*.

## 5-3: Make the 3-point

5-3 isn't as good an opening roll as 3-1 or 4-2, for an obvious reason. There are *two* gaps between the 3-point and the 6-point, so the 3-point doesn't form as effective a block:

Diagram 23. Black has played 5-3

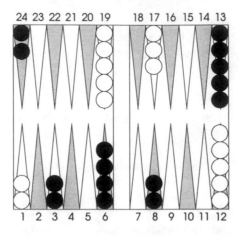

Still, the 3-point is an inner board point, and there's no better way to play this roll.

## 6-1: Make the bar-point (7-point)

This roll is a little stronger than a 5-3, about on a par with a 4-2.

**Diagram 24. Black has played 6-1**

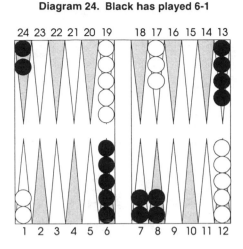

By making the *bar-point*, Black has succeeded in creating a block three points long. In backgammon, long blocks of consecutive points are called **primes**, and one key goal is to build a prime and trap your opponent's men behind it. With the 6-1 roll, Black is well on his way to making a prime. The only drawback to this roll is that the 7-point is not an inner-board point, so it doesn't help keep White from entering if you send him to the bar.

### 6-5 Lover's Leap: Play From Your 24-Point to the Midpoint
6-5 is a special roll, since it's the only number that lets you get a back checker all the way to the security of your midpoint (the 13-point). This is a good roll, although not quite as good as starting with a point-making throw.

**Diagram 25. Black has played 65**

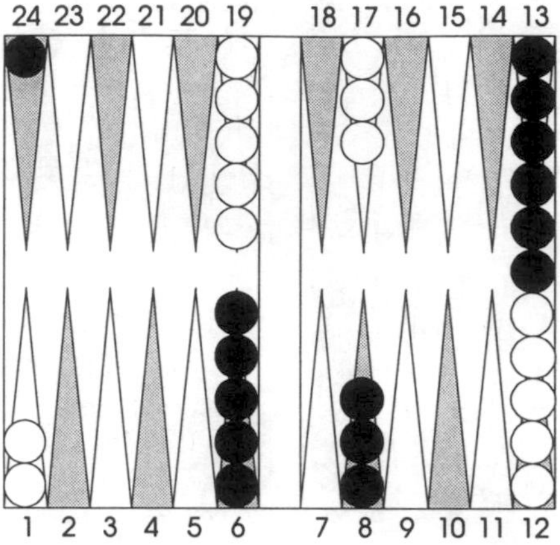

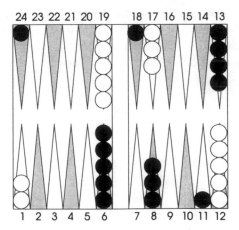

## The Bar-Point Split Plays:  6-2, 6-3, and 6-4

Now we're going to look at rolls that can't be played by simply making new points. These rolls require a little more creativity and imagination. We're going to play these rolls the same way.

**Diagram 26. Black has played 6-2**

**6-2**

As you see, we recommend a very bold play with 6-2: one checker from the 24-point to the 18-point, and one checker from the 13-point to the 11-point. Black opens up three blots around the board. Why?

In the answer lies the essence of dynamic backgammon: Black has no way to play this number safely, so instead he's placing his checkers directly on the points he *wants* to make. In effect, he's challenging White to a fight: "Hit me if you can, he's saying, "but in return I may just hit you back."

Black can gain from this play in two ways: White might throw a poor number next turn and miss Black's blots altogether. Although White can hit with sixes and ones, he misses with twos, threes, fours, and fives. So it's by no means certain that he can hit at all. Even if he does hit, he'll probably have to leave blots of his own. Then Black might enter from the bar and hit those blots. An exchange of hits like that could leave Black well ahead in the race.

Of course, White might roll perfectly. For instance, he might roll a 6-1 and make the 18-point with checkers from the 12-point and the 17-point, sending your checker to the bar to boot! That's a risk you take when you play dynamically. You give your opponent a few chances to smash you with great rolls, while in return you have a good chance to make substantial progress.

**6-3, 6-4**

With 6-3 and 6-4, you should make similar plays. Wth 6-3, play one checker from the 24-point to the 18-point, and another from the 13-point to the 10-point. Wth 6-4, play one checker from the 24-point to the 18-point and one from the 13-point to the 9-point.

**Diagram 27. Black has played 6-4**

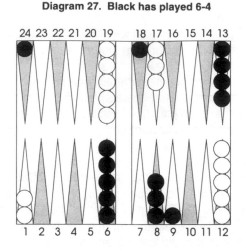

The alert reader will have noticed that Black had another play with 6-4: he could have made an inner board point by playing from the 8-point to the 2-point and from the 6-point to the 2-point. Why did we reject this play?

To see why, take a look again at our comments to the 5-3 play. We pointed out there that the gaps between the 3-point and the 6-point made a formation that was not so effective for blocking. The same is true for making the 2-point, only more so. The 2-point is so far from the 6-point and 8-point that it has little, if any, blocking value. This leads to another rule of thumb in backgammon: *beware of making your 1-point and 2-point early in the game.* Checkers on these points are away from the main scene of the action, and can easily become liabilities instead of assets.

### The Building Plays: 5-4, 4-3, 5-2, and 3-2.

I like to call these rolls the **building plays**. Except for **5-4**, all of these rolls could be played completely safely. With **4-3** and **5-2**, Black could play a checker all the way from the 13-point to the 6-point. With **3-2**, Black could play from the 13-point to the 8-point. In many parts of the world, or among groups of beginners, it's not uncommon to see these rolls played in just that fashion.

But that's not the dynamic way - the winning way. I prefer to use the rolls to prepare to make good points next turn. If my opponent can throw a perfect shot and hit me, more power to him. I won't be out of the game. But if I get away with these plays, I'll be building up my position quickly. That's the way I like to play - full steam ahead. Let's look at the best way to play these rolls.

### 5-4: Play 24-point to 20-point, and 13-point to 8-point.
My play of the **5-4** gets me ready to make an anchor on the **20-point** next turn:

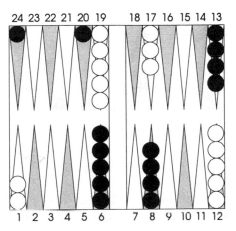

Diagram 28. Black has played 5-4

### 4-3: Play 24-point to 20-point, and 13-point to 10-point.
I love this roll. It leaves three blots, but I have plenty of possibilities next turn. Playing 24 to 20 prepares to make the anchor on the **20-point**, while 13 to 10 gives me many combinations to make the 4-point or the 5-point.

34

Diagram 29. Black has played 4-3

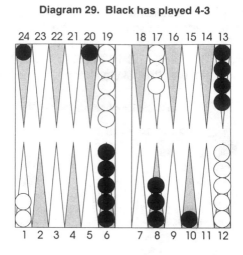

**3-2: Play 13-point to 10-point, and 13-point to 11-point.**
Another roll which takes a small risk for some real building potential down the road:

Diagram 30. Black has played 3-2

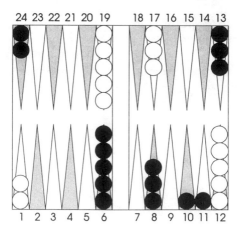

It's not so easy for White to hit those two blots, while almost all of Black's rolls will make a new point next turn. (Try them and see.)

**5-2: Play 13-point to 8-point, and 13-point to 11-point.**
This is the least effective of the building plays:

Diagram 31. Black has played 5-2

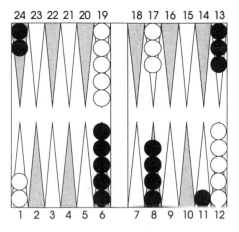

Black takes a small extra risk this turn, for a few more possibilities next turn.

### The Slotting Rolls: 2-1, 4-1, and 5-1.

With these plays, I advocate a really aggressive play: use the larger number to pull a man off the 13-point, and with the ace, slot the 5-point! **Slotting** means placing a blot where your opponent can hit it with a single number - in this case a 4. For instance, I play an opening 2-1 like this:

**Diagram 32. Black has played a 2-1**

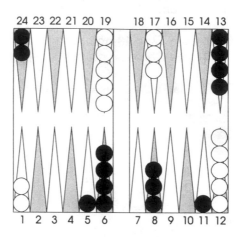

At first glance, this looks crazy. I've put a blot where my opponent can hit it with a 4, and if he hits it, I lose a lot of ground in the race to get my checkers around the board. Why would I take such a risk?

Basically, for two reasons. First of all, if my blot isn't hit, I have a great chance to cover it next turn. When I do that, it's as though I started with the best roll of all, a 3-1. Second, being hit and sent back isn't the end of the game. I can still reenter, build a defensive position, and hope to hit a **shot,** an opportunity to hit a blot, as my opponent comes around the board. The more you play backgammon, the more you'll learn that it's very difficult to avoid leaving **shots** for the whole game. And a player whose whole game is built around playing safe will rarely be a big winner.

Here's a secret that very few beginners understand: *in backgammon, taking calculated risks isn't really risky - in the long run, it's actually the percentage play.*

That's it. Those are all the rolls that you can start the game with, and the dynamic way of playing them. You can play these openings with confidence. When you run up against a player who likes to play completely safe, piling his checkers up on the points he already owns, don't worry. He may look askance at your bold style of play, but in the long run, you'll win his money.

# V. SAMPLE GAME 1 - WINNING STRATEGY

The best way to see how backgammon should be played is to take a look at some actual games. You'll get a feel for what a game looks like, from start to finish, and we'll introduce some sound principles of play as we go along. We've also included plenty of diagrams, so you won't get lost along the way. If you have a backgammon board, take it out now and set it up as we showed back in Diagram 2 - the starting position. Then follow along with the game. Be sure to take the time to actually make the moves on your board - you'll find that this greatly enhances your understanding.

In our first game, the White pieces are conducted by a player of the old school - conservative and cautious. Black is a player who understands the new dynamic style.

**1. Black rolls 4-3: plays 24-point to 20-point and 13-point to 10-point.**

**Diagram 33. Black has played 4-3**

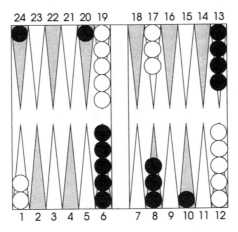

Excellent! Black didn't roll one of his best numbers, but he still made the most of his roll. By playing 24 to 20, Black stakes a claim on the 20-point, one of the most valuable points on the board. If White doesn't do anything, Black will hope to roll a 4 and make this point next turn. In addition, the checker on the 20-point now looks out over White's entire outerboard (the points from the 18-point to the 13-point). If White tries to leave a blot in this area, Black will have good chances to hit it.

The checker on the 10-point is also usefully placed, increasing the chances that Black will be able to make a blocking point next turn. Take a look: If Black's next roll is a 6-4 or a 6-2, he will be able to make the 4-point. If he rolls a 5-1 or a 5-3, he can make the 5-point. And if he rolls a 6-3, he can make the bar (7)-point. That's five new rolls that play effectively next turn because Black took a small risk this turn. That's dynamic backgammon: small risks now to earn big rewards later.

**2. White rolls 4-1: Plays 12-point to 16-point and 16-point to 17-point**

Diagram 34. White has played 4-1

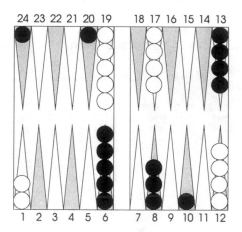

White, on the other hand, plays very conservatively. While his play is perfectly safe (it leaves no blots), it's also completely unconstructive - White is no closer to building a new point or escaping his back men than he was at the beginning of the game.

Did White have a better play? I think so. In his position, I would have made this play - 19-point to 20-point, hitting Black's blot, and 1-point to 5-point. Take a look at how this move looks:

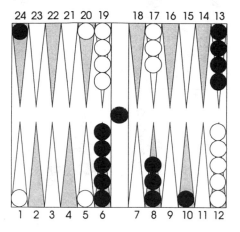

**Diagram 35. White has played 4-1 the recommended way**

See the difference? White is now attacking both 5-points: Black's (the 5-point) and White's (the 20-point). In addition, Black is on the bar, and will have to enter that checker before he can do anything else. Sure, Black may be able to enter and hit White somewhere. But if he doesn't, he's in serious trouble, and even if he does, so what? The game is just getting started and there's a lot of play to come. At least this way, White has made some progress toward a couple of his goals. Next turn, he might be able to make the 5-point, the 20-point, or both.

Now go back to the position in Diagram 34, and we'll look at Black's next roll in the actual game.

**3. Black rolls 3-1: Plays 8-point to 5-point and 6-point to 5-point, *making the 5-point.***

40

Diagram 36. Position after Black plays 3-1

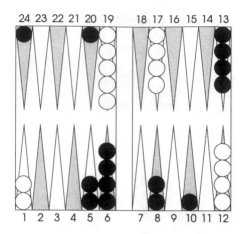

A nice roll, although notice that Black had many nice rolls in this position. That's another advantage of Black's dynamic style of play: it creates positions where a lot of rolls play well. When you play in this style, your opponents may complain about how lucky you are. Let them. You concentrate on winning.

Black's roll was so good that you may have noticed that there were a couple of other useful points that he could have made. For instance, he could have used his roll of 3-1 to make the 7-point (with the checkers on the 8-point and 10-point) or the 20-point (by moving up the checker on the 24-point). Why did he pick the 5-point instead of one of these other plays?

Let's take the possibilities one by one. He picked the 5-point over the 7-point because, although both are blocking points, the 5-point is also an *inner*-board point. That means it will help keep White on the bar if Black can score a hit. He picked the 5-point over the 20-point because he feels it will be relatively easy to make the 20-point next turn, or, if need be, to run the checker from the 20-point over to Black's **outfield** (in the area of the 9, 10 and 11-points).

The 5-point, on the other hand, might be hard to make, since Black only has a few throws each turn which can make it. In this case, with two possible goals, Black chose to make the one that was *harder* to do, leaving the relatively easy one for later. That's a good rule to remember.

## 4. White rolls 5-4: Plays 12-point to 17-point and 12-point to 16-point.

Diagram 37. White has played 5-4

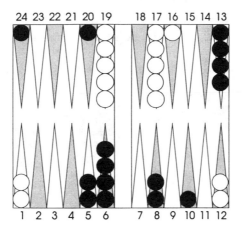

A bad roll for White, which forces him to leave a blot somewhere. His play is all right, although playing 12-point to 21-point was also OK.

## 5. Black rolls 6-4: Plays 20-point to 16-point, hitting White's blot, and continues on to the 10-point.

Diagram 38. Black has played 6-4, hitting

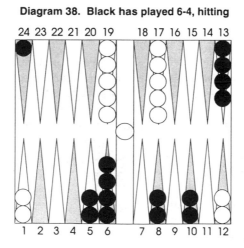

42

A great shot for Black, which accomplishes three objectives at once: hitting White, escaping one of his back checkers, and making a new point. It's hard to do more with a single roll. White's passive play has led him into serious difficulties.

**6. White rolls 3-1: Plays bar to 3-point, and continues on to the 4-point.**

**Diagram 39. White has played 3-1 from the bar**

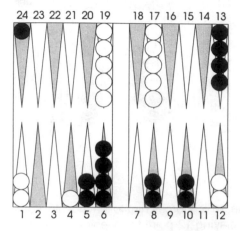

Remember that when you have a checker on the bar, you *must* reenter that checker before you can move any other checker. Since White rolled 3-1, the first half of his move had to be one of two plays: either use the 1 to enter, by playing bar to 1-point, or use the 3 to enter, by playing bar to 3-point. White chose the latter. That left him with a 1 to play, which he decided to play with the checker he had just entered. Legally, however, he could have used this one with any of his other checkers, had he wanted to.

This roll shows the other drawback of being hit. Not only did White lose ground in the race, but he lost the opportunity to use the roll constructively. Normally, he would have used the 3-1 to make the 20-point with checkers from the 19-point and the 17-point, but here he didn't have that opportunity.

At this point, it should be clear that Black has an advantage in the game. He's built two new points, the 5-point and the 10-point; he's escaped one of his two back checkers, while White has lost ground and now has three checkers back instead of two; and he's well ahead in the race to come home. Many players might let this opportunity slip by, but not Black!

### 7. Instead of rolling, Black doubles to 2!

Remember what we said in the section on doubling earlier in this book. To double, Black picks up the cube, turns it to the face labelled **2**, places it on White's side of the board, and says, *I double.* (Sneering is optional.) Now it's up to White to *drop*, and concede one point, or *take*, and play on with the value of the game doubled. A game would now be worth two points, a gammon, four points, and a backgammon, six points. However, once he has accepted the cube, White cannot be doubled again. He gets to play the game out to the finish, or until the advantage swings his way and he gets to redouble Black!

### Doubling Guidelines

When should you offer a double, and when should you take a double? This is one of the most difficult, perhaps *the* most difficult, decision in backgammon. Doubling and taking doubles requires tremendous judgement and experience, and you'll find that the longer you play the game, the more your knowledge of doubling deepens and expands. But here are a few guidelines:

• You should be willing to take a double if you have at least a 25% chance of winning the game, and you're unlikely to lose a gammon or a backgammon. This fact comes as a surprise to many people, since at first it seems that you wouldn't want to take a double if you're an underdog. Why play for more if you can just give the game up? But that's not the right way to look at the situation.

To see where the 25% number comes from, consider this example: suppose you were in a position that you knew you could win just one time in four. Suppose you sat down to play this position four times against another player, and he started each game by doubling you. Here's what could happen:

If you dropped each of the four doubles, you would lose four games at one point per game. Net loss: four points.

If you took each of the four doubles, you would lose three games and win one. At two points per game, you would lose six points in the three games you lost, and win two points in the one game you won. Net loss: four points - exactly the same as if you dropped!

That's why 25% is the break-even point for accepting doubles. If you have a better chance than that, you should take, and with worse chances, you drop.

• How big a favorite should you be to double? That's a good question, and there's a lot of disagreement about this question, even among the best players. (That's part of what makes backgammon such an interesting and exciting game - there's so much that isn't yet understood, even among the acknowledged grandmasters.) Most players feel that the side contemplating a double should be at least be a 2-1 favorite, or even a little better. Aggressive players like to double a little earlier than this, while some conservative players try to get very close to the 75% mark before doubling.

Now let's get back to our game. We listed Black's advantages a little while ago. Black feels that the sum total of these advantages makes him at least a 2-1 favorite to win the game, so he doubles. What should White do?

## 8. White Accepts the Double
White decides that he can win this position at least 25% of the time, so he takes the double. Why did he think that? Answer - he guessed, based upon his experience in playing positions of this sort. As you play backgammon, you will build up experience and make your own decisions about the strength of certain formations. There are no cut-and-dried formulas for deciding questions of this sort. Players just make their own best judgments.

Was White correct? I don't think so. Although Black's game is not yet overwhelmingly strong, White has as yet nothing going for him. I think it's too hard for White to turn the game around quickly, and I like to give up such positions. Still, many reasonable players might disagree with this assessment. At any rate, White's take means we have an interesting game ahead of us.

## 9. Black rolls 6-2: Plays 10-point to 4-point, hitting, and 6-point to 4-point.

Diagram 40. Black has played 6-2

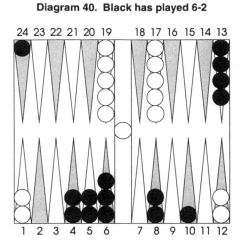

Black's second great shot in a row.  Now White is really in trouble.  There is no disagreement on how to play this roll.  Any time you can make an inner-board point and hit your opponent at the same time, you should do so.

**10. White rolls 2-2: Plays bar to 2-point, 17-point to 21-point, and 19-point to 21-point.**

Diagram 41. White has played 2-2

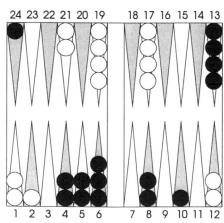

White finally builds an inner-board point, which was a long time coming. In part, this was a result of White's ultra-conservative opening strategy. It's difficult to build points without being willing to take some risks in the opening.

Although this was a good roll by White, it doesn't change the fact that Black has a very big advantage. In fact, if Black were to double in this position, White would have a mandatory pass.

**11. Black Rolls 5-4: Plays 24-point to 15-point.**

Diagram 42. Black has played 5-4

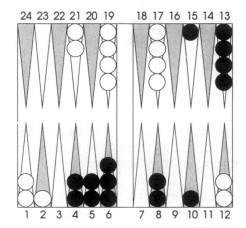

Not an especially good roll. Black would have liked a 6-4, which he would have played 8-point to 2-point and 6-point to 2-point, making a point *on White's head,* or perhaps a 6-3, which he would have played 13-point to 7-point and 10-point to 7-point, making a *5-point prime.* His roll of 5-4 is not completely useless, however. By running to the 15-point, he is preparing to escape his last checker.

### Duplication Strategy
This play also illustrates a principle known as **duplication**. Here's how it works. White would like to hit one of the two Black blots in the position. The Black checker on the 15-point can be hit by the White checkers on the 12-point, but White needs to throw a 3 on one die or the other to hit.

Now look at the Black checker on the 10-point. That can be hit by the White checkers on the 1-point and 2-point, but only if White throws a particular combination of numbers. The only combinations that will work are 6-3 (to hit from the 1-point) and 5-3 (to hit from the 2-point). Notice that these two rolls both contain a 3, the same number that White needed to hit from the 12-point.

In backgammon parlance, we say that *White's 3s are duplicated.* He needs the same number to hit on one side of the board as the other, which ensures that most of White's dice combinations (all those that don't contain a 3 on either die) *won't* hit. That's good news for Black, bad news for White.

If, while playing a game, you can duplicate your opponent's good numbers as much as possible, you'll ensure that he has fewer useful numbers to play. In the long run, that means more winning games for you, and fewer for him.

**12. White rolls 6-4: Plays 17-point to 23-point and 19-point to 23-point.**

**Diagram 43. White has played 6-4**

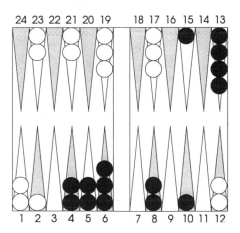

White misses his shot, but is able to build another point in his inner board. However, this was a costly miss. Black has now escaped his last rear checker, one of the key goals of successful strategy. Black's also far ahead in the race, so to win, White will have to hit a last-ditch shot as Black brings his men home. The next few moves should be a period of consolidation. Black will try to bring his men home safely, hopefully making his 3-point and 7-point in the process.

White will fill in the gaps in his own home board, hoping to hit a shot much later in the game.

**13. Black rolls 6-3:  Plays 13-point to 7-point and 10-point to 7-point.**

Diagram 44. Black has played 6-3

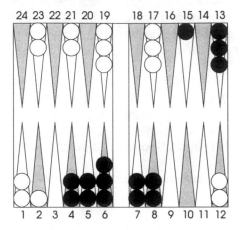

An excellent play by Black. Notice that this is not the safest play. Black could have played 15-point to 6-point, or 15-point to 9-point and 13-point to 10-point, either of which would have left White fewer chances to hit a Black blot than the play he made.

Black was willing to leave White a direct shot at his checker on the 15-point because he understands the tremendous power of the five-point block (or prime) that he created with his play. Suppose that White hits the blot on the 15-point next turn. How is the game likely to go from that point? Black will soon reenter his checker on White's inner board. White may be able to hit again, but Black will quickly escape.

Meanwhile, White's three checkers on the 1-point and 2-point are stuck. White will need to roll some aces and deuces to reach the 3-point, then several sixes to jump over the five-point prime. It's not very likely that this will happen, so Black feels that the risk that White will roll a three, hit him, and somehow win from that point is justified.

## 14. White Rolls 55: Plays 12-point to 22-point with two men.

### Diagram 45. White has played 5-5

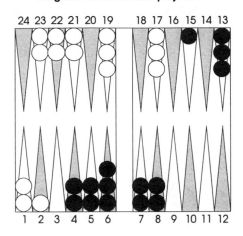

To the novice, this might look like a good roll. White advances 20 pips in the race and makes an inner board point besides. In fact, it's a poor roll, not just because White missed the blot on the 15-point, but because White is advancing too quickly.

But you ask, "If backgammon is basically a racing game, how can anyone be advancing too quickly? The faster, the better, right?" Not quite. Backgammon is much complex than just a simple racing game. That's part of what makes it so fascinating.

Here's what I mean: if both sides had broken all contact between their checkers, and were just racing home with their men, then big rolls would always be better than small rolls. But if one side is trapped, as White is in this position, and is waiting for the chance to hit a shot later in the game, then he wants to roll small numbers at this stage of the game. He wants to make up the points in his board gradually, so that his home board is fully made up *just as he hits the shot he is waiting for.*Then, he can keep the checker he hit on the bar while he brings the remainder of his men around to join them. If he moves too quickly at this stage of the game, his board will form and then disintegrate *before* he hits a shot, and he will lose anyway. (In fact, we'll see that very scenario happen in this game.)

## 15. Black rolls 6-4: Plays 15-point to 9-point, 13-point to 9-point.

Diagram 46. Black has played 6-4

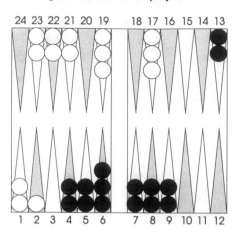

Notice that Black could have used this roll to make the 2-point (8-point to 2-point and 6-point to 2-point) but this play is much stronger. He has now completed a full 6-point prime, one of the chief goals of middle game strategy. Notice that no matter what numbers White rolls, there is no way his men on the 1-point and 2-point can escape Black's blockade *so long as Black's prime remains intact*. Since the largest number on a die is six, there's no roll that will hop over a 6-point prime. White is trapped for the time being.

Does this mean White has no chance to win? No, although his chances are now quite small. Since Black has to bring all his men into the home board in order to bear off, he will have to break up his prime in the near future. This process is called *rolling the prime home*, and how well Black performs this task affects his winning chances substantially.

## 16. White rolls 4-3: Plays 17-point to 20-point and 17-point to 21-point.

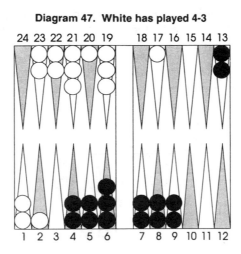

**Diagram 47. White has played 4-3**

A straightforward play. White hopes to roll a 1 or a 3 next turn and make the 20-point, giving him a very strong home board.

**17. Black rolls 6-2: Plays 13-point to 5-point.**

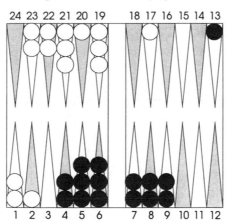

**Diagram 48. Black has played 6-2**

Another straightforward play. Black's next goal is to make the 3-point, if necessary giving up the 9-point in the process. If he makes the 3-point, he will have a full six-point prime from the 3-point to the 8-point, so the 9-point will be superfluous.

**18. White rolls 5-3: Plays 17-point to 20-point, and 19-point to 24-point.**

### Diagram 49. White has played 5-3

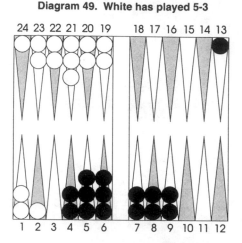

White has achieved a strong home board. If Black didn't have a prime, and White were in position to hit a blot, his home board might easily keep that checker trapped long enough for White to win. Unfortunately, there's no blot to be seen, and White's board will not last long.

**19. Black rolls 6-3: Plays 9-point to 3-point and 6-point to 3-point.**

**Diagram 50. Black has played 6-3**

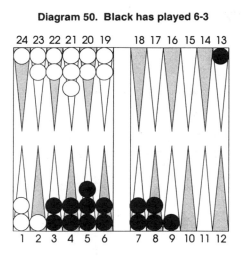

A great shot. Black *rolls his prime* forward one pip. Black's blot on the 9-point is quite safe, as there are no sevens on the dice!

**20. White rolls 5-4: Plays 19-point to 24-point and 19-point to 23-point.**

**Diagram 51. White has played 5-4**

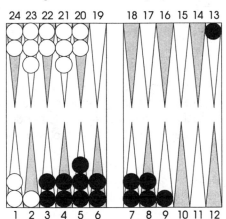

*There goes the neighborhood* as Billy Horan (one of backgammon's strongest grandmasters) is fond of saying.

**21. Black rolls 3-2: Plays 9-point to 7-point and 5-point to 2-point, hitting.**

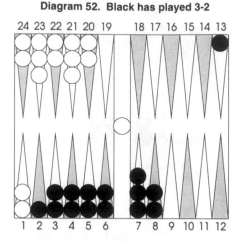

Diagram 52. Black has played 3-2

Black hits, even though White could roll a two and hit him right back. Bold play? Not at all. Since Black has a full 6-point prime, White can never escape. It may take Black some time to enter a checker from the bar if he is hit, but it won't matter, since his prime cannot break while he is on the bar.

**22. White rolls 5-4: No play.**
White can't move, since Black owns both the 5-point and the 4-point. Remember that if you are on the bar, you must enter the checker before you can move any other checkers. In this case, White needed to roll either a one or a two on the dice to enter, since those are the only open points in Black's home board.

**23. Black rolls 6-6: Plays 13-point to 7-point, and 8-point to 2-point with two men. Cannot play fourth six.**

### Diagram 53. Black has played 6-6

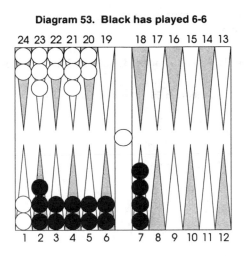

When you roll a double, you get to play that number four times, *if possible*. In this case, Black has only three legal plays of a six. The checkers on the 7-point cannot move six pips, because White owns the 1-point. In backgammon lingo, his sixes are *killed*.

**24. White rolls 4-1: Plays bar to 1-point, and 20-point to 24-point.**

### Diagram 54. White has played 4-1

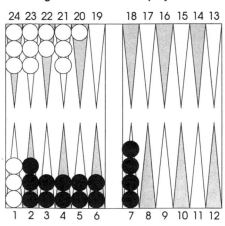

A forced play. White has managed to enter from the bar, but loses another home board point in the process.

**25. Black rolls 4-3: Plays 7-point to 3-point, and 7-point to 4-point.**

Diagram 55. Black has played 4-3

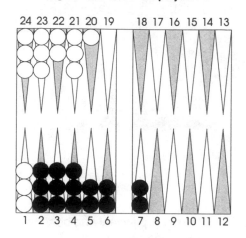

Remember that Black can't bear off any men until *all* his checkers are in the home board (points 1 through 6). His last task before the bearoff is to bring the four checkers on the 7-point into his home board somewhere. With this roll, he brings in two of the checkers.

**26. White rolls 5-3: Plays 20-point to 23-point with the 3; cannot play a 5.**

Diagram 56. White has played 5-3

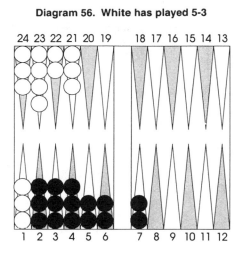

White has no legal way to play a 5, since his checkers on the 1-point are blocked, and there are no checkers on the other side of the board that can move five spaces. In that case, he only has to play a 3, which he does.

**27. Black rolls 5-5: Plays two checkers from 7-point to 2-point, then bears off two checkers from the 5-point.**

Diagram 57. Black has played 5-5

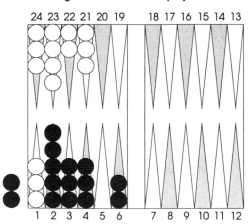

Black plays his first two fives from the 7-point to the 2-point. Once he has done this, he has all 15 checkers in the inner board, so he is entitled to start bearing off checkers. With his two remaining fives, he removes the two checkers on his 5-point.

**28. White rolls 6-2: Plays 1-point to 9-point.**

Diagram 58. White has played 6-2

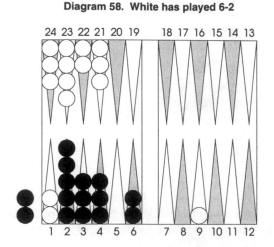

Now that Black has **broken** his 7-point, White is once again free to move sixes.

**29. Black rolls 6-5: Bears off a checker from the 6-point; no legal 5 to play.**

**Diagram 59. Black has played 6-5**

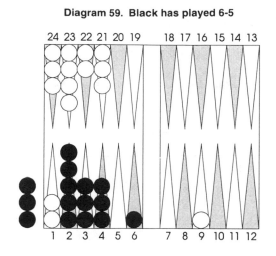

Look at this position carefully to make sure you understand what has happened. Black used the six to bear off one of his checkers from the 6-point. He would normally use the 5 to bear off a checker from the 5-point, but there are no more checkers on the 5-point. If White didn't still own the 1-point, Black could use his 5 to play 6-point to 1-point, but that's impossible here. So Black has no way to play the 5, and gives up that part of his roll.

## 30. White rolls 3-2: Pays 9-point to 14-point.

**Diagram 60. White has played 3-2**

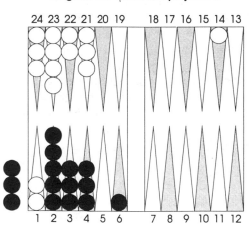

Too bad! White had some winning chances if he could have hit Black's blot by throwing any number containing a 5, or the combination number 4-1. As is, he has nothing better than to bring his checker in the outfield closer to home.

**31. Black rolls 6-5: Bears off a checker from the 6-point and a checker from the 4-point.**

Diagram 61. **Black has played 6-5**

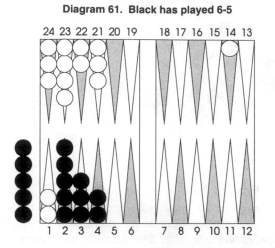

Look at this play closely and compare it to Black's last play. These situations cause some confusion for newcomers to the game. This turn, Black uses the 6 to bear a checker off the 6-point, as you might expect. Then, since Black has a 5 left to play and no checkers on the 5-point or 6-point he is able to use the 5 to bear off from the next highest point, in this case the 4-point.

Why couldn't he bear off from the 4-point last turn (move 29)? Because in that case he still had a checker on a point higher than the 4-point. *You can only bear off from a point with a higher number than the point itself if all the higher points have been cleared of checkers.* Study these two examples carefully, and you'll avoid any confusion at the table.

**32. White rolls 3-2: Plays 14-point to 19-point.**

**Diagram 62. White has played 3-2**

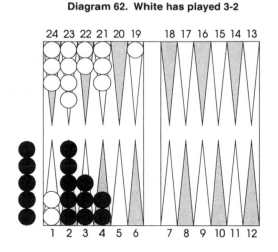

White is piddling along. Not only is he very unlikely to win the game, but there is now a real possibility that he could lose a gammon. Remember, if your opponent bears *all* his men off before you bear off *any* men, you lose a gammon, or twice the value of the doubling cube. Since the cube is now on 2, White will lose four points if he loses a gammon!

**33. Black rolls 6-2: Bears off a checker from the 4-point, and plays 4-point to 2-point.**

**Diagram 63. Black has played 6-2**

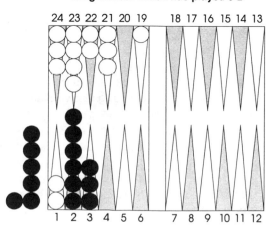

Since Black has no checkers on the 5-point or the 6-point, he can use any 4, 5, or 6 on the dice to bear off from the 4-point.

You may ask, "Why didn't he take two men off, by using the 2 to bear off from the 2-point?" That would have been perfectly legal. However, it would have left a vulnerable blot on the 4-point, which White could then have hit if he rolled any 3. Black avoided this possibility by **picking up** the blot on the 4-point.

**34. White rolls 4-3: Plays 1-point to 8-point.**

### Diagram 64. White has played 4-3

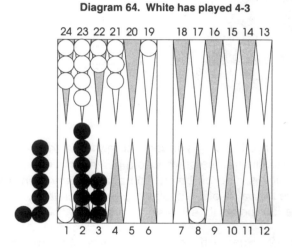

White has little choice on his moves any longer. He must start running his back checkers out to try to avoid losing a gammon.

Why not move both back men, by playing 1-point to 5-point and 1-point to 4-point? Because White still has chances of hitting one of Black's blots, which would still give him some chances of winning the game. If Black's next roll is 6-5, for example, he will have to bear two men off the 3-point, leaving a blot there which White could hit. If you take a look at Black's position, you will find that almost half his numbers leave a shot next turn. (Count them!)

**35. Black rolls 6-1: Bears a checker off the 3-point with the six, and plays 2-point to 1-point, hitting White.**

**Diagram 65. Black has played 6-1**

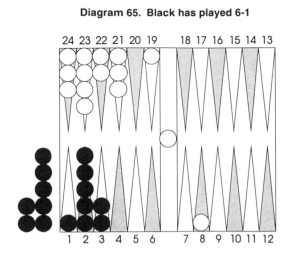

Black had to leave another shot (his only other legal play with the ace was to play 3-point to 2-point), so he made the most aggressive play, putting White on the bar.

**36. White rolls 4-2: Plays bar to 4-point and continues on to the 6-point.**

**Diagram 66. White has played 4-2**

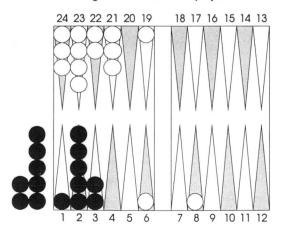

White's winning chances are now gone. There's no way he can win the race, now matter how well he rolls or how poorly Black rolls. But we continue playing, because it's not decided whether Black will win a single game (worth 2 points) or a gammon (worth 4 points).

### 37. Black rolls 2-2: Bears four men off the 2-point.

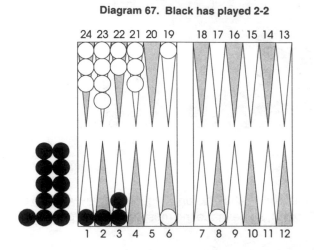

Diagram 67. Black has played 2-2

A great roll for Black, and now the gammon looks quite likely.

### 38. White rolls 5-1: Plays 8-point to 13-point, and 6-point to 7-point.

**Diagram 68. White has played 5-1**

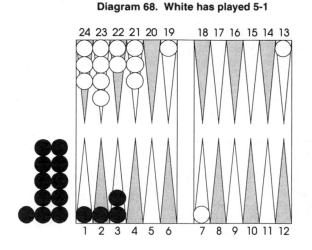

Take a look at that ace that White just played. It may look insignificant, but that accurate play might have saved White two more points! Remember what we said before in our chapter about the rules - if one side bears off all its checkers while the other side has no checkers off and at least one checker in the other side's home board, that's a triple game, or backgammon. With the cube on two, a backgammon is worth six points! So by moving that last checker out of Black's inner board, White has avoided the possibility of losing a triple game.

**39. Black rolls 6-3: Bears off two men from the 3-point.**

**Diagram 69. Black has played 6-3**

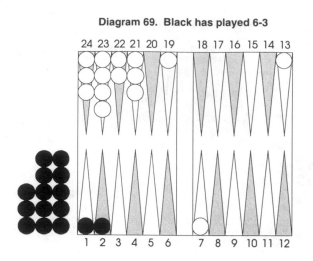

Forced play.

**40. White rolls 4-4: Plays 7-point to 19-point with three fours, and 13-point to 17-point with the last four.**

**Diagram 70. White has played 4-4**

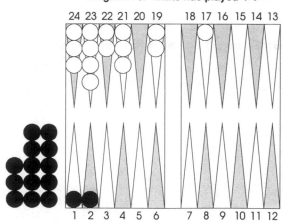

That last roll moved a lot of freight, but not quite enough to save the gammon.

In the final position, Black doesn't even have to roll. Even his smallest number (2-1) will bear off his last two checkers, so he just claims a gammon, and writes **plus-4** on the scoresheet.

There's our first look at a real backgammon game. Play through it two or three times for practice. You'll find that your knowledge of the backgammon rules is greatly strengthened. Also, some of the plays in the game, which may have looked strange at first glance, will now start to make more sense to you.

## Sample Game Summary
What really happened in this game? Black made several dynamic plays in the early game, and White responded passively. As Black's plan came to fruition, White found himself trapped in what is known as an **ace-point game** - a position in which one player is trapped on their opponent's ace-point, hoping to hit a shot in the late stages of the game. As you play backgammon, you'll see a fair number of ace-point games, and you'll eventually learn to play them properly from either side.

Now let's move on and look at a completely different type of game.

# VI. SAMPLE GAME 2 - THE BLITZ!

Up to now, we've described moves in a pretty lengthy fashion, so as to be crystal clear. In most books, backgammon moves aren't described this way, because it takes up too much space and is clumsy to read. Instead, games are recorded in **backgammon notation**. It was first invented by Paul Magriel, one of backgammon's greatest players and writers, back in the 1970s.

---

**Here's how backgammon notation works:**
• Instead of saying **Black rolls 3-2** we'll just write Black 32.
• Instead of saying **13-point to 10-point**, we'll write 13/10.
• If an opposing blot is hit, we put an asterisk after the play, like this: **12/6\***.
• If two men move from one point to another, we'll say this: **20/16(2)**.
• If a checker enters from the bar, we'll write **Bar/20**.
• And if a player bears off a checker, we'll write **3/off**.

---

The example above looks like this in standard backgammon notation: **Black 32: 13/10, 8/6\***. Quite a savings in space, and just as clear, once you get used to it. Set up your board in the initial position, and follow along.

1. **White 64:** 1/11
2. **Black 55:** 6/1\*(2) 8/3(2).

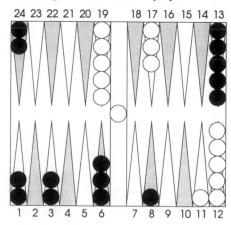

Diagram 71. Black has played 55

With his opening 64, White ran out to the 11-point. That wasn't our recommended play back in our chapter on dynamic openings, but it's a common way of playing the roll, and you'll see it a lot.

### The Blitz
Black was hoping to hit this checker by rolling a 2, but instead he rolls a 55. To play the 55, he uses checkers from the 6-point and the 8-point to make two of his inner board points in one swoop, putting White on the bar at the same time. This is a very aggressive way of playing double-fives, and it starts a new type of game which we haven't seen before, called the **blitz.**

In a blitz (sometimes called an **attacking game**), one side tries to close his inner board very quickly, before the opponent can establish an anchor anywhere. This game plan can only be tried if your opponent has broken the anchor he started with, back on the one-point.

As long as your opponent retains the anchor on the one-point, he has no blots for you to hit. Once he breaks that anchor, the blots he creates become vulnerable to attack.

When a blitz works, your opponent gets a checker or two trapped on the bar before he's had a chance to develop his game at all; the result is usually a gammon for you. When it fails, the other player usually gains a steady advantage, because you've moved your checkers too far forward too quickly. It's a double-edged game plan, suitable for players with an aggressive style. Let's see how it works in this game.

### 3. White 66: No move
With Black owning his 6-point, White is stuck on the bar and can't enter. This rolls illustrates some of the power of an early attack. White throws one of his very best numbers, which would normally make him a significant favorite in the game, and instead has to waste it completely.

### 4. Black: Doubles to 2
A **blitz** is a powerful game plan, and Black wastes no time in doubling the stakes. He's already a favorite in the game.

### 5. White: Takes the double
White's in some trouble, but he still has plenty of chances to win. All top players would agree with this take.

### 6. Black 62: 13/7, 13/11*

**Diagram 72. Black has played 62**

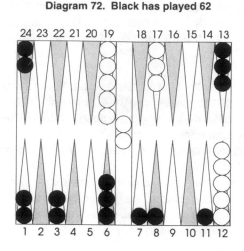

24 23 22 21 20 19   18 17 16 15 14 13

1 2 3 4 5 6   7 8 9 10 11 12

With this roll, Black's blitz is in full swing. White now has two checkers stuck on the bar, while Black has moved an impressive array of **builders** into position to make the open points in his board.

### 7. White 65: Bar/5

Since the 6-point is occupied, White can only enter one checker, using the 5 he rolled. This was not a good roll, since Black can hit this checker with any combination of ones, two, threes and sixes.

### 8. Black 63: 11/5*, 8/5

A good shot by Black. He uses to builders to make the 5-point *on White's head*. Black has now strengthened his 3-point board to a 4-point board, and White is in serious trouble.

**Diagram 73. Black has played 63**

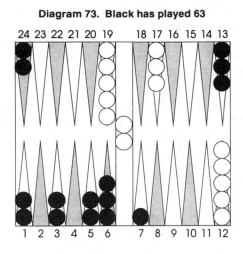

### 9. White 53: No move

Once again, White rolls a number that does not enter either checker from the bar, since Black has made both the 3-point and the 5-point.

### 10. Black 64: 13/7, 13/9

**Diagram 74. Black has played 64**

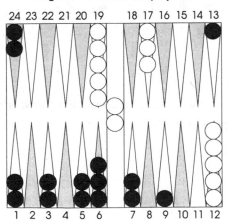

More ammunition! At this point Black is not concerned with his own back checkers. He's throwing all his energies into the blitz, trying to close out White's two checkers before White can gain a foothold. If he succeeds, he'll be able to escape his own back checkers at his leisure. If he fails, it won't matter very much whether Black shuffled his back men a little or not.

Remember the Foreman-Ali fight in Zaire? Foreman used all his energy trying to knock Ali out in the first few rounds. That's analogous to what Black is trying to do here. If Black's knockout punch fails (as did Foreman's) then the advantage will swing quickly back in the other direction.

**11. White 43: Bar/4**

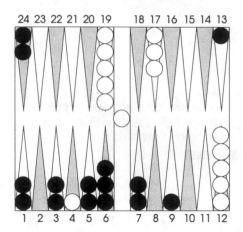

Diagram 75. White has played 43

White was hoping to throw fours or twos. He threw a single four, which enabled him to enter one of his two men.

**12. Black 54: 9/4* 13/9**

**Diagram 76. Black has played 54**

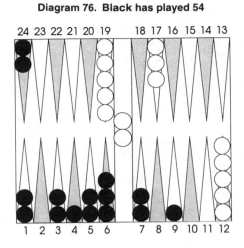

Black had another choice here. He could have made his 2-point, by playing 7/2, 6/2. Many players would have chosen that move, which gives Black a five-point inner board. However, if White then throws *any* four, he has his anchor and the security that it offers. Black is trying as hard as he can to prevent White from ever making any anchor at all. With that in mind, he aims to hit any White checker that lands in his board. It's all or nothing for Black at this point.

**13. White 52: Bar/2**

**Diagram 77. White has played 52**

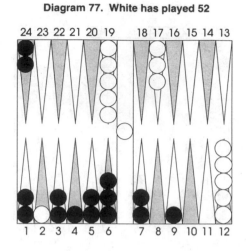

White wanted to roll a four and hit back. Black would then lose time bringing that checker in, and White would have a better chance of anchoring. But at least White was able to get one checker in. Now he has a chance to anchor if he throws a two next turn.

**14. Black 52: 7/2\*, 4/2**

**Diagram 78. Black has played 52**

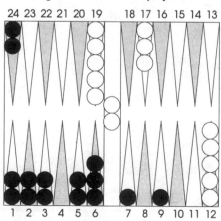

Excellent play by Black! He had a couple of chances to go wrong here. One possibility was playing something like 9/4 and 24/22. This makes a five-point board, but doesn't put White on the bar. That's too passive. White could roll a two, anchor on the 2-point, then win the game later on.

Another possibility was 6/4 and 7/2*. This makes a 5-point board and leaves White on the bar with both men, but it exposes Black to a direct return shot from the bar. If White rolls a two in response, he hits Black and slows down his attack. Black's actual play was much better. He hits White, puts two checkers up in the air, makes a 5-point board, and doesn't expose any blots to a return shot. It's the perfect combination of aggression and safety.

### 15.  White 64:  Bar/4

**Diagram 79. White has played 64**

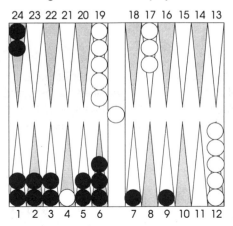

White's still fighting.

### 16.  Black 43:  7/4*, 24/20

**Diagram 80. Black has played 43**

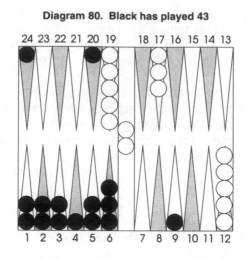

Black hits, of course, with the three. What about the four? There's no way he can improve his blitzing possibilities with the four, because he already has his only two spare checkers within range of the 4-point: the checker on the 9-point and the checker on the 6-point. Now it's time to get the back checkers moving.

## 17. White 54: Bar/4*

**Diagram 81. White has played 54**

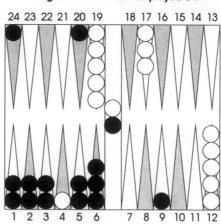

Ouch! Finally White hits a shot from the bar. Will he roll another four and put an end to Black's attack?

**18. Black 64: Bar/21, 20/14**

Diagram 82. Black has played 64

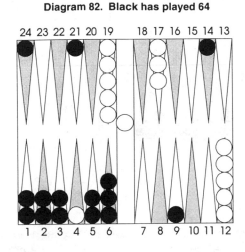

Black can't use the 6 to enter, since a 6 takes him to the 19-point, which is blocked. So Black has to enter with the 4, on the 21-point. That leaves him with a 6 to play, which he uses to move the checker from the 20-point to the 14-point. The 14-point is 10 pips away from the 4-point, so Black now can hit on the 4-point with rolls totalling 10: 6-4 and 5-5. In fact, by moving out to the 14-point, the roll of 5-5 next turn will actually close the 4-point, assuming, of course, that White stays out.

**19. White 52: Stays out. A bad shot for White.**

**20. Black 55: 14/4\*, 9/4, 21/16.**

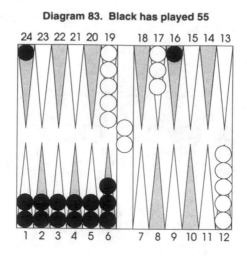

**Diagram 83. Black has played 55**

Success! With this excellent shot, Black finally succeeds in closing the board. Now Black has only a few technical problems to overcome to secure the gammon. Notice that there is no longer any need for White to roll until Black eventually opens up an inner board. With all the points 1-6 occupied, White can't enter no matter what number he rolls.

## 21. Black 63: 24/15

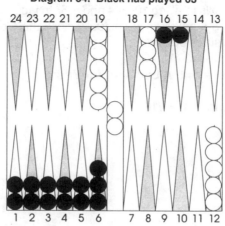

**Diagram 84. Black has played 63**

Black's correct strategy is to bring his two back men out together. He's trying to avoid being in a situation where rolling a big double (like 5-5) would cause him to open up points in his home board because his back checker is blocked. When he can move his two back men beyond White's midpoint, this possibility will disappear.

**22. Black 41: 16/11**

**23. Black 65: 15/10, 11/5**

**Diagram 85. Black has played 65**

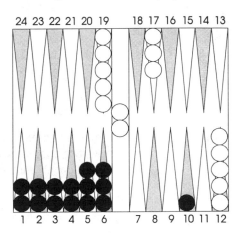

According to plan. Black has succeeded in **breaking contact**, and in a moment he will start his bearoff. If he can avoid being hit as White tries to come in, he will almost certainly win a gammon.

**24. Black 52: 10/3**

**25. Black 61: 6/off, 5/4**

**Diagram 86. Black has played 61**

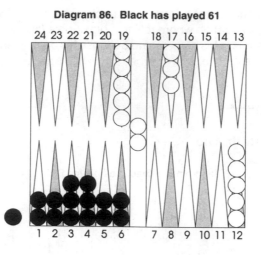

The safest way to bear off is to try and remain even on the highest points in your home board. That way, you can remove two checkers from the last point without leaving a shot. (If you had three checkers on your last point, removing just two of them would leave a costly blot.) Black's last play leaves him with two men on his 6-point, and a total of four men on his 6-point and 5-point combined. This is a safe formation. We'll soon see an example of the danger of not remaining even on the high points.

**26. Black 63: 6/off, 6/3**

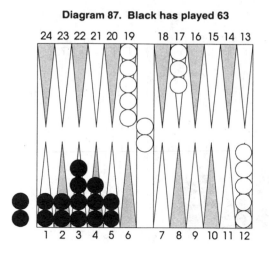

**Diagram 87. Black has played 63**

Black could take two men off by playing 6/off, 3/off, but this would leave a blot on the 6-point that White could hit by rolling a six. Instead, he correctly plays that blot to the 3-point, leaving himself safe for this turn.

Since Black has finally opened a point in his board, White gets to roll again.

**27. White 54: Stays out**

**28. Black 65: 5/off(2)**

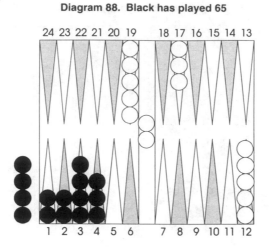

Diagram 88. Black has played 65

A forced play. Since Black has no checkers on the 6-point, he uses the six to bear a checker off the next highest occupied point, the 5-point. He then uses the five to bear the other checker off the 5-point.

### 29. White 51: Bar/5

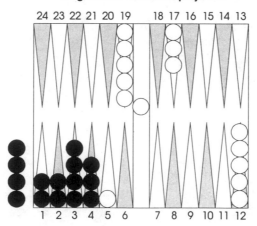

Diagram 89. White has played 51

With the five, White can enter on the newly opened 5-point. The ace-point is still blocked, so he can't enter there.

### 30. Black 64: 4/off(2)

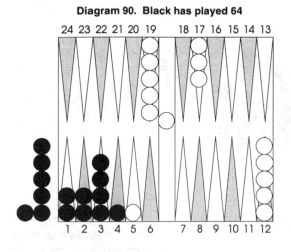

**Diagram 90. Black has played 64**

Oops! With this roll Black is forced to remove two of the three men on his 4-point. That shows why it's so important to keep an *even* number of men on the highest point when you're bearing off. Now White is back in the game if he can roll a four.

### 31. White 43: Bar/4*, 12/15

**Diagram 91. White has played 43**

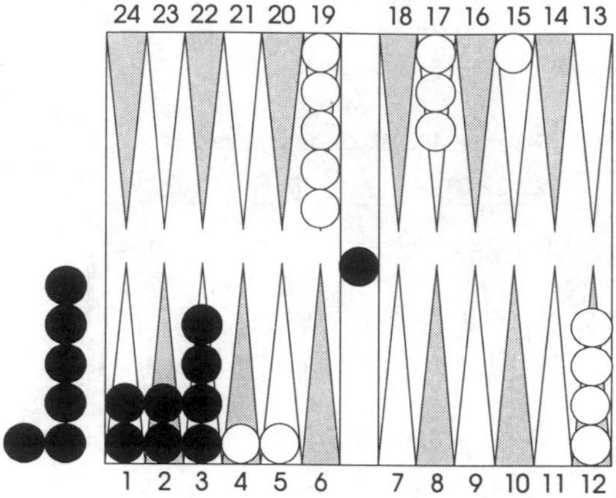

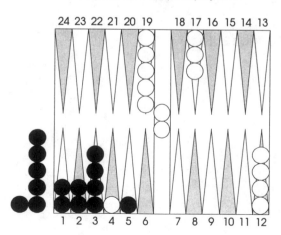

That's exciting! White hits a last-ditch shot, and now the game enters a new phase. White will try to build some points and hopefully trap the Black checker behind a blockade. If he succeeds, he'll certainly save the gammon and may even win the game.

## 32. Black: 55: Bar/20/15*/10/5*

**Diagram 92. Black has played 55**

What a shot! At a backgammon tournament, this is the kind of roll that has the spectators screaming and sends the players into ecstasy or despair, depending on which side of the table you're on. Many years ago, one of backgammon's all-time great players and writers, Barclay Cooke, called backgammon "the cruelest game". It's rolls like this, just when White thought he had crept back into contention, that Cooke had in mind.

Of course, the game's not over yet. White can still roll a five and get back into contention.

### 33. White 61: Bar/6
Not this time. Now it looks like White really is finished.

### 34. Black 51: 5/4*, 4/off

**Diagram 93. Black has played 51**

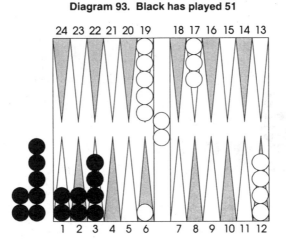

Many players would automatically play 5/off, then look around for their best ace, which would be 3/2. But Black's play is perfectly legal and considerably better. Remember that you're allowed to play your two numbers in any order, *as long as you play your entire roll.* Black has played his ace first, 5/4*, and then uses the five to bear off his checker from the 4-point, since he has no checker on a higher point. That's considered to be a legal and complete play of a five.

Why hit this checker when Black essentially has the gammon wrapped up? Black is greedy - he wants to win a backgammon worth 6 points (with the cube on 2) and not just 4 points for a gammon. Backgammon is a very seductive game (much like real life, some say) and offers many chances to be greedy, some justified, some not. You be the judge here.

**35. White 53: Bar/5**

**36. Black 63: 3/off(2)**

**37. White 43: Bar/4/7**

**Diagram 94. White has played 43**

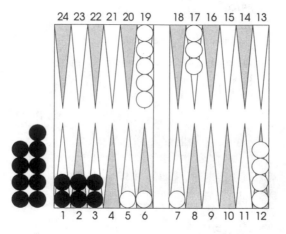

Now the outcome is settled. Even if Black throws a double next turn, nothing can prevent White from moving the men on the 5 and 6-points into Black's outer board, thus avoiding the backgammon. At the same time, there's no way Black can fail to win a gammon.

Result: four points to Black.

# VII. MORE BACKGAMMON PLAY

## CHOUETTES
The simplest way to play backgammon is to sit down against a single opponent and play for an afternoon or evening. If you join a backgammon club, however, you may often find that several people all want to play at once. Rather than break into several separate games (which would leave someone out if the number of players was odd), players will organize what is called a *chouette*. A **chouette** is just a way for several people to participate in one game of backgammon. It is a more social way of playing, very popular at backgammon clubs around the country.

To start a chouette, all the players roll for high dice. The player with the highest dice is the **box**. The player with the second highest dice is the **captain**. All other players are part of the **team**, and they assist the captain. The box now plays a game against the captain, with the members of the team joining the captain in the play. The captain, however, rolls the dice and has the final say on all plays. The captain and all players on the team have separate cubes, all of which begin the game at the 1-level.

All players control their own doubling cube. When it is the box's turn, he may elect to double the captain and all the team members, or just certain players, or no one. If several players are doubled, they each make separate decisions on whether to take or drop. When the captain is *on roll*, players can decide individually to double the box or not.

If the box beats the captain, he retains the box for the next game, whether or not he beats the other players. If the captain wins, he becomes the box for the next game and the former box player moves down to the bottom of the line. All other players move up, with the second player on the team becoming the new captain. Players can leave or join a chouette at any time. A new player starts at the bottom of the rotation.

## CLUBS AND TOURNAMENTS
The best way to meet other backgammon enthusiasts is at a backgammon club or a backgammon tournament. There are many clubs around the country, usually at least one in every major city. Clubs meet once or twice a week in a hotel or a restaurant and usually run small tournaments where

beginners can get started.

There are also many backgammon tournaments at the local, regional, national, and even international level. Regional tournaments in the United States usually attract between 100 and 200 players, and are held over a long weekend. International tournaments are gala affairs, with hundreds of participants from around the world, black-tie dinners, main and side events, and prize funds which can reach hundreds of thousands of dollars.

The two most prestigious events in the world are the World Championship, held every July in Monte Carlo, and the World Cup, held every other year in an American city. The winners of these tournaments are usually among the world's very best players.

For a complete and current list of clubs around the United States, write to: The Gammon Press, P.O. Box 294, Arlington, MA 02174. Include $1 for postage and handling.

## MAKING FURTHER PROGRESS

That brings us just about to the end of this book. If you're like most people, you probably want to go out and try your hand at this game. That's good: go to it. If you can't find enough players in your town, teach some of your friends to play. They might be reluctant at first. Don't worry, that's natural. Most folks are a little leery about trying new things. Keep after them, and chances are that pretty soon you'll have a group of players just as avid as you are.

What's next? If you like reading, there's a lot of books about backgammon and its finer points. You'll see ads for a few at the end of this book.

If there are organized clubs and tournaments in your area, pay them a visit. You won't have to play at first - most clubs welcome newcomers, and they won't mind if you just sit and watch. Ask the director who the best players are, then go and observe their game. Try to pick up some pointers by watching what they do. If you have questions, it's not such a good idea to ask the players themselves. Some people get quite intense while they're playing, and don't always welcome questions from the spectators. Ask a director, or, if there's a crowd watching, one of the other spectators. After that, it's up to you.

Good luck!

# VIII. Glossary

**automatic double** - An optional rule to increase the stakes in game. If both players roll the same number on the dice to start the game, they may agree to turn the doubling cube to "2" for that game before rolling over.

**backgammon** - A triple game, which occurs when one player bears off all his checkers while his opponent still has at least one checker on the bar or in the first player's home board. Also, the name of the game.

**bar** - The raised vertical strip running down the center of a backgammon board. Checkers which are hit are placed on the bar, and must reenter the game in the opponent's inner board before any other checkers can be moved.

**bear off** - removing checkers from the board. A player can only bear off after all 15 of his checkers have been moved to his inner board.

**blitz** - A game plan which involves attacking the opponent's checkers and trying to build a closed home board at the same time.

**blot** - A single checker on a point, which is vulnerable to being hit by the opponent.

**checkers** - The playing pieces. Each side has 15 checkers to start the game.

**olocod board** Λ oituation whoro ono playor hao mado tho oix pointo in hio homc board. If he then hits one of his opponent's checkers, that checker will not be able to reenter the game until the first player opens up ("breaks") his home board.

**doubles** - Rolling the same number on both dice. Doubles allow the player to move that number four times.

**doubling cube** - The large die numbered "2" through "64" in powers of 2. The doubling cube controls the number of points at risk in the game.

**gammon** - A double game, which occurs when one player bears off all his checkers while his opponent fails to bear off any checkers.

**hit** - Moving to a point where the opponent has only one checker ("blot"). The hit checker is placed on the bar.

**home board** - The six points for each player which are the jumping-off locations for the bearoff. In our diagrams, Black's home board are the points labelled 1-6; White's home board are the points 19-24.

**points** - The triangular markers on a backgammon board; also, two or more checkers together on the same point, which constitute a "made point".

**prime** - A series of consecutive blocking points. A "full prime" is six points in a row.

**quadrant** - One of the four quarters of the backgammon board.

**single game** - The simplest and most common form of victory, which occurs when a player bears off all his checkers while his opponent has borne off some, but not all, of his checkers.

**slot** - To deliberately place a blot on a point, hopimg to make that point on a future roll.

# POSITRONIC WINNING BRIDGE SOFTWARE
(for IBM compatibles)
**Two Great Software Programs to Choose From**

**IMPROVE YOUR BRIDGE SKILLS** - These fun and **easy-to-play** user-friendly programs feature **beautiful state-of-the-art color graphics** for EGA and VGA monitors allows you to play against the computer while learning as you use the practice and help keys.
**ENDORSED BY THE WORLD'S BEST PLAYERS!** Tony Forrester says, *The game you can teach to be as good as you are.* Eric Kokish says, *Positronic Bridge will give you the battle of your life.*

## BASIC BEGINNER POSITRONIC BRIDGE - $49.95

**UNIQUE CHALLENGE!**
Designed for novice bridge players, provides **real simulation** of actual play. Numerous options include: rubber or duplicate bridge play; standard bidding; simple signaling; practice and play modes; random deals or keyboard input; show or hide opponents' hands; plus other exciting features.

**ARTIFICIAL INTELLIGENCE**
Unique **built-in artificial intelligence** capability, the latest, most **exciting** feature, **automatically improves** the games' skill level as you improve, so the game is **always a challenge.** As you get better, the game gets better!

## POSITRONIC INTERMEDIATE COMPETITOR - $99.95

**POWERFUL CAPABILITIES!**
Designed for bridge club members at novice to intermediate levels, this challenging version **includes all the conventions and bidding systems** experienced players expect: weak, strong and variable notrump bidding; 5 card Major or ACOL systems; count and attitude signals; and rubber and duplicate scoring.

**CHALLENGE AND COMPETE!**
Expert bidding system interface allows play against the best bidding systems man can create. Think you're a good player? Challenge the Competitor and get better.

---

## BECOME A BETTER BRIDGE PLAYER!
*Thinking Software for Thinking Players*

**Yes**! I'm ready to take the Positronic challenge and match my skills against these exciting games! Enclosed is a check or money order to:
Cardoza Publishing
P.O. Box 1500, Cooper Station, New York, NY 10276
Please include $4.50 postage and handling for U.S. and Canada, other countries $9.00. Outside United States, money order payable in U.S. dollars on U.S. bank only.

ITEM DESIRED _____

(Circle One)     Basic Beginner Positronic Bridge ($49.95)     Positronic Intermediate Competitor ($99.95)     BACK

NAME _____

ADDRESS _____

CITY _____ STATE _____ ZIP _____

# KASPAROV CHESS TRAVELLER™

*SAITEK - The World Leader in Intelligent Electronic Games*

**POWERFUL AND FUN** - 34 level/setting combinations including 16 playing levels makes an unbeatable choice for beginning and casual players. Convenient, economic and powerful (8K program), the Kasparov Traveller™ actually makes some very real human errors. Even beginners have a chance to win! Knows all common chess rules and has features like 6 full move take-backs. Suggests moves if you get stuck, rejects illegal moves.

**GREAT TRAVEL COMPANION** - Ideal as a travel chess computer, its easy to learn and use. Knows all common chess rules and has features like 6 full move take-backs. Turn off at any time and continue play later - computer remembers position.

To order, send just $69.95 for the Kasparov Chess Traveller

# KASPAROV CHESS GK2000™

*SAITEK - The World Leader in Intelligent Electronic Games*

**TOP OF THE RANGE** - This fabulous chess computer has outstanding full features, and a very high speed program all combined with ease-of-use. Rated at a 2100 ELO Performance!

**POWERFUL FEATURES** - 64 levels of play including sudden death, tournament, beginners' playing levels. Shows intended move and position evaluation, take back up to 30 ply, user selectable book openings library: choose from Active, Passive, Tournament, complete book, no book. Great table-top design - full info LCD. Choose between high speed Selective Search or powerful Brute Force program.

To order, send $169.95 for the Kasparov Chess GK2000

# PRO BRIDGE 310

*SAITEK - The World Leader in Intelligent Electronic Games*

The world's most innovative **hand-held** bridge computer challenges you like never before! Designed in a sleek, ergonomic design, this authentic and **innovative** game can be taken anywhere for fun and learning - **ideal** for anyone who enjoys a **great game** of bridge.

**GREAT FOR LEARNING AND ENTERTAINING** - *Saitek's* Pro Bridge, designed to give **beginning and intermediate** players a **challenging** & **competitive** game, plays Standard American 5 card majors and ACOL. A large, **easy-to-read** LCD display and **32 keys** provide you with a wealth of information and **many options.**

**GAME COMES READY TO PLAY** - The Pro Bridge's innovative LCD screen shows your own and dummy's hands clearly; keeps score; shuffles and deals cards automatically; follows suit, and can even show all four hands simultaneously.

**PACKED WITH OPTIONS** - At the **touch of a key**, check on number of tricks made, contract and currently set bidding system; other keys allow you to claim remaining tricks; shows the rubber to date, both above and below the line. You can pass, double, redouble, rebid and more.

**EXTRA FEATURES** - Here's just a few of the **many extras** you'll find in this **exciting** game:
• The **latest in innovative sound effects** that create the noise and atmosphere of a bridge game. Optional key turns on and off the effects.
• Can be linked to 510 unit for two player, two computer play!

To order, send $229.95 by check or money order to:

Cardoza Publishing,
P.O. Box 1500, Cooper Station,
NY, NY 10276

# BRIDGE SHADOW
*SAITEK - The World Leader in Intelligent Electronic Games*

This compact LCD computer bridge game is easy-to-use and **fits into the palm of your hand**! Take this **exciting** game anywhere for fun, learning and non-stop bridge challenges.
**GREAT FOR LEARNING AND ENTERTAINING** - Ideal for **beginning and casual players**, the Bridge Shadow entertains while coaching. **Power-packed 16K program** plays Standard American 5 card majors and has an **on-line help key** to coach you in the proper moves.
**EIGHT LEVELS OF PLAY** - This versatile **hand-held** game allows you **eight different levels of play;** from beginning to intermediate. You not only **select** the skill level desired, but also bidding aggressiveness.
**THE GAME THAT HAS IT ALL** - Ideal for bridge players, the Bridge Shadow's **innovative LCD screen** shows your own and dummy's hands clearly; keeps a running score; shuffles and deals cards automatically; and can even show all four hands simultaneously.
**AMAZE YOUR FRIENDS** - Your friends will be amazed as your game gets better and better, especially when they learn how much fun you're having while improving!
**Also included** is a Bridge introduction showing all the rules of the game for fast reference.

To order, send $119.95 by check or money order to:

Cardoza Publishing,
P.O. Box 1500, Cooper Station,
NY, NY 10276

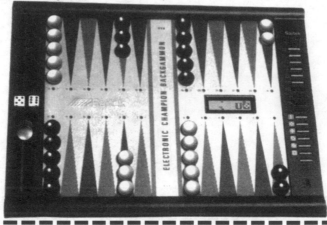

# LCD CHAMPION BACKGAMMON
*SAITEK - The World Leader in Intelligent Electronic Games*

**CHALLENGE THIS GREAT HAND-HELD BACKGAMMON GAME** - This pocket-sized handheld champion, **winner** of the Computer Olympiad - is fun, exciting and ready to play. **Great for travel** - fits into your pocket, briefcase or sports bag. Take it anywhere you go!

**GREAT GAME FEATURES - Easy** to play: the LCD display **shows full game board** - no need to worry about losing pieces; directional key enters moves; computer automatically rolls the dice (or roll yourself - dice supplied); offers, accept or reject doubles; **computer remembers game** - turn on to resume play. You can even set-up your own games!

**10 LEVELS OF SKILL, 3 STYLES OF PLAY** - The **power and versatility** of this 32K program is amazing! Computer emulates styles of actual human players with **30 different combinations** of playing strength and aggressiveness, 10 levels of skill and 3 styles of play. Build up your confidence from beginner to winner.

**FEATURES, FEATURES AND MORE FEATURES!** This **amazing** game has a built-in coach and tutor and can suggest best moves available . It allows take-back, rejects illegal moves and **even plays against itself.** LCD shows evaluation of position, the chances of a blot being hit and the **complete** game statistics and score!

**WANT MORE?** - 4 games in one! Play Backgammon, Jacquet, Tric Trac and Moultezim! Try to beat the computer or use the coach at the same time to improve your game!

To order, send $139.95 plus postage and handling to:
Cardoza Publishing, P.O. Box 1500, Cooper Station, New York, NY 10276

# POWER BACKGAMMON STRATEGY
## 2 Master Books - Unbelievable Value

---

### Bill Robertie's Inside Winning Strategies - Now Available!

**A MUST FOR SERIOUS PLAYERS!**
*This is the strategy package serious backgammon players must have!* You'll receive these two great strategy books, Advanced Backgammon Volume 1: Positional Play and Advanced Backgammon Volume 2: Technical Play, musts for players looking to win.

**LEARN FROM THE WORLD'S GREATEST PLAYER!**
Go from beginner to winner! Bill Robertie's powerhouse package is designed to take you all the way. This **tremendous** course, personally written by two-time world champion Bill Robertie, is packed with **winning information** in **easy**-to-follow steps, shows you how to raise your level to competitive and even **expert club play**.

**BILL ROBERTIE'S COMPLETE WINNING COURSE**
For the **serious** backgammon player, the new editions of these two big volumes cover the full gamut of expert play. You'll learn positional play, opening, middle and back games; blitzes and priming games; technical play, endgames, races and bearoffs, and even advanced checker and cube play.

**LEARN HOW TO THINK AND PLAY LIKE A PRO**
Each strategy is explained in words and shown in examples and sample games so you understand the concepts and reasoning behind every strategy play. Each page is jam-packed with insights, diagrams and the thinking that goes into every move. With brilliant analysis throughout, you'll be winning more than ever before and will rise to new levels!

**550 SOLID PAGES/TWO MANUALS**
The best advanced strategy on backgammon ever written gives you two bound books containing over 550 pages of solid winning information.
To order, send $59.95 plus postage and handling to:
Cardoza Publishing, P.O. Box 1500, Cooper Station, New York, NY 10276

---

### 2 FOR 1 OFFER!!!

Yes! I want to take advantage of this **2 for 1** offer and be a great backgammon player. Please **rush** me the **Power Backgammon Strategies**, including both big books. Enclosed is a check or money order payable to Cardoza Publishing for $59.95.

Cardoza Publishing
P.O. Box 1500, Cooper Station, New York, NY 10276

Please include $4.50 postage and handling for U.S. and Canada, other countries $9.00. Outside United States, money order payable in U.S. dollars on U.S. bank only.

NAME _____

ADDRESS _____

CITY _____ STATE _____ ZIP _____

**30 Day Money Back Guarantee**

BACK